FREDERICA

Its Place in History

FREDERICA:

COLONIAL FORT AND TOWN

Its place in history

by TREVOR R. REESE

Illustrated by Peter Spier

Published by
Fort Frederica Association
in cooperation with
Fort Frederica National Monument
National Park Service
United States Department of the Interior

St. Simons Island, Georgia, 1969

CONTENTS

16104

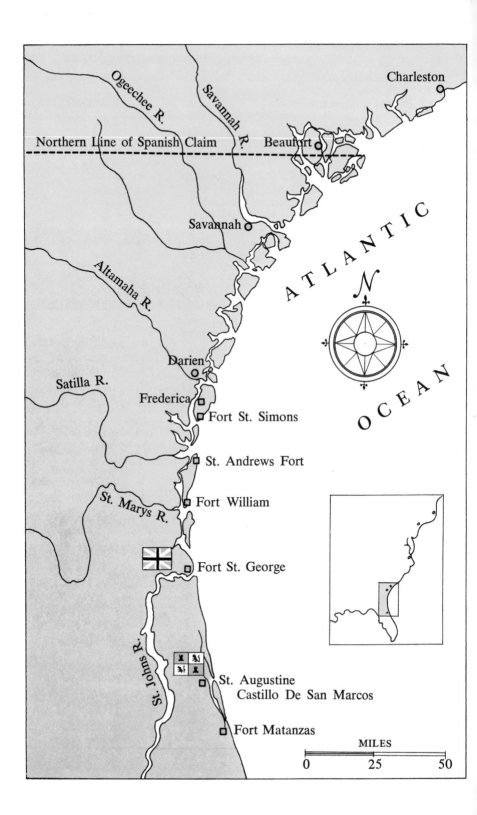

Charleston

Ogeechee R.

Savannah R.

Northern Line of Spanish Claim

Beaufort

Savannah

ATLANTIC

Altamaha R.

N

Satilla R.

Darien

OCEAN

Frederica

Fort St. Simons

St. Andrews Fort

St. Marys R.

Fort William

Fort St. George

St. Johns R.

St. Augustine
Castillo De San Marcos

Fort Matanzas

MILES

0   25   50

Foreword

For many years the Fort Frederica Association has sought to gather together pertinent information about Frederica in one concise story. The late Margaret Davis Cate assembled a mass of Frederica data in the form of maps, books, booklets and articles, some of which she wrote. This collection is now housed in the Margaret Davis Cate Memorial Library at Fort Frederica and was a valuable source of material for this booklet.

Through the National Park Service, we were fortunate to secure the services of Dr. Trevor R. Reese of the Institute of Commonwealth Studies in London, England, to write the story and to have Mr. Peter E. Spier of New York prepare the layouts and illustrations.

In *FREDERICA: Colonial Fort and Town—Its Place in History,* Dr. Reese has captured the "spirit of Fort Frederica" and put it into brief, readable form.

The Association, in conjunction with the National Park Service, is proud to publish this work that will be most interesting and helpful to the casual visitor to the Frederica area as well as to the student of Colonial history.

Alfred W. Jones
President, Fort Frederica Association

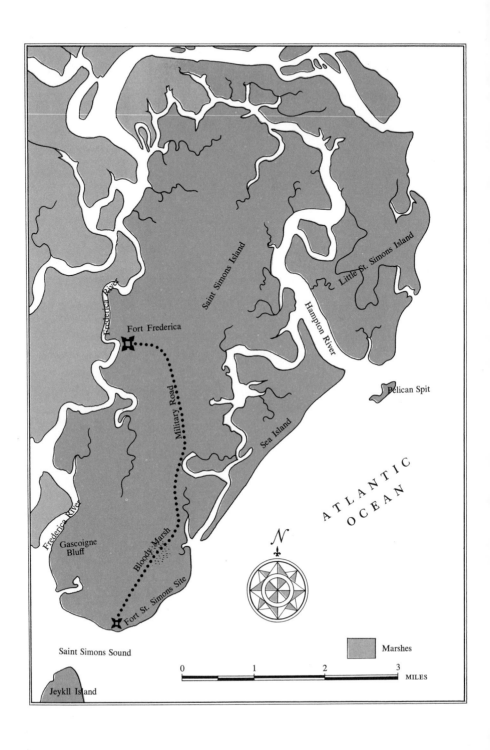

Little St. Simons Island

Saint Simons Island

Frederica River

Fort Frederica

Military Road

Hampton River

Pelican Spit

Sea Island

Frederica River

Gascoigne
Bluff

Bloody Marsh

ATLANTIC
OCEAN

N

Fort St. Simons Site

Saint Simons Sound

Jeykll Island

Marshes

0   1   2   3
                              MILES

PREFACE

This short account is intended to place the story of the old town and fort of Frederica in its historical setting. For this purpose, I have examined records both in Great Britain and Georgia, but the account inevitably owes much also to intensive research and excavation by several American scholars, who in recent years have checked and augmented the information available in the original documents upon which all Georgia historians base their work. No one can write about Frederica and the Golden Isles of Georgia without finding himself greatly in the debt of the late Mrs. Margaret Davis Cate, who made the subject her own and left a magnificent collection of material, both primary and secondary, in the library that bears her name at the Fort Frederica National Monument. During my stay on St. Simons Island, Mr. William H. Glover, the superintendent at the Monument, was a wise and friendly counsellor, and Mrs. Ruby Berrie and Mrs. Shirley Collins were patient and co-operative in enabling me to make the fullest use of the library's facilities. These, and other persons connected with the National Park Service and the Fort Frederica Association, all helped to kindle an affectionate interest in a fascinating area of Georgia history.

T. R. R.

Institute of Commonwealth Studies
University of London: May, 1968

ORIGINS

Frederica was strategically the most important of the early settlements in Georgia. It was the hub of the colony's defence against the Spaniards to the south, and in 1742 it was the headquarters of the forces which decisively repulsed a Spanish invasion. Frederica's very success in this role in the war against Spain, however, signalized the beginning of its own decline, for with the Spanish danger removed and the security of Georgia assured, the town's *raison d'etre* was lost and its demise hastened.

Frederica owed its name to the English royal family, which in the seventeenth and eighteenth centuries was a popular source for the nomenclature of overseas settlements. Thus, Virginia originated as Sir Walter Raleigh's compliment to the virgin queen, Elizabeth I; Carolina was a derivation of King Charles II, and Maryland a derivation of his queen, Henrietta Maria; New York took the title of the duke who became, briefly and disastrously, King James II. For the southernmost and last of the thirteen original colonies, the name Georgia was chosen in honour of the reigning monarch, George II, and it was a measure of the significance attached to the settlement at Frederica that it should have been named after the heir to the throne, Frederick Louis, Prince of Wales, only son of the King and father of George III. The good-natured Frederick was popular with the English people, but he was detested by his father, labelled "Poor Fred" by later historians, and on his premature death became the subject of the much-quoted epitaph beginning:

Here lies Fred
Who was alive and is dead.

The epitaph's conclusion was that since it was only Fred who was alive and was now dead—"There's no more to be said." In the case of the unfortunate prince, this was possibly true. In the case of the town that bore his name, however, an illustrious, if short, history earned the esteem of all the British colonies in America in the eighteenth century, and inspired scholars and enthusiasts of later generations to study it in detail and restore its ruins as a public monument and living memorial to a minor, but glorious, episode in the development of Georgia and colonial America.

The establishment of Frederica in 1736 was the natural corollary of the foundation of Georgia in 1732. The three principal motives for creating the new colony were, first, to relieve Great Britain of an insolvent, unemployed, and unwanted section of its population; second, to increase the contribution made by the colonies to the commerce and resources of the British Empire; and third, to strengthen the security of South Carolina and the southern frontier of the colonies against the French and Spaniards, an objective which, if it was to be adequately achieved, clearly necessitated the early establishment of a frontier post such as Frederica.

Ever since the settlement of the Carolinas in the middle of the seventeenth century, England and Spain had contested the ownership of the land between St. Augustine in the south and Charleston (S. C.) in the north. The boundaries of England's southern colonies had never been defined satisfactorily, and alarms and frontier incidents were common. As early as 1720 the British Government had ordered the construction of a fort near the mouth of the Altamaha River, though the one that was built at that time (Fort King George) had a chequered history and was eventually abandoned. The major step in cushioning the southern colonies against attack was the decision in 1732 to found a colony in the territory lying between the Savannah and Altamaha rivers. In order to put the new settlement plan into effect, a corporation was constituted under the name of the Trustees for Establishing the Colony of Georgia in America. The Trustees were authorized to legislate for the colony's government over a period of twenty-one years, after which it reverted to the Crown.

A party of 114 emigrants left England on 17 November 1732 in a 200-ton frigate. Leadership of the party was entrusted by the Trustees to one of their own number, James Edward Oglethorpe, a man of thirty-six, in the prime of an active life. Oglethorpe and the migrants reached America in January 1733 and soon established the town of Savannah, the administrative centre and principal port of early Georgia. Other towns and villages were quickly started: at Ebenezer, farther up the Savannah River; at Highgate, about five miles to the south-west of the first settlement; at Purysburgh, about twenty-two miles away on the South Carolina side of the river; at Vernonburgh, a little below Savannah; and at Abercorn, about fifteen miles above. All these settlements were in the north of the colony, but in early 1736 some Scottish families established Darien, on the north bank of the Altamaha, sixteen miles above St. Simons Island and along the southern frontier facing Spanish territory. A few months later, the fortified town of Frederica was founded on the west side of St. Simons Island.

Frederica was situated on a bluff washed by the Frederica River, then known as the South Branch of the Altamaha, before it passed to the ocean through Jekyll (now St. Simons) Sound. The island is twelve miles long and three miles wide, and lies some sixty air miles south of Savannah among the so-called Golden Isles of the Georgia coast. Sir Robert Montgomery, a Nova Scotia baronet, had referred to these islands twenty years before in a pamphlet expatiating on the benefits to be gained from colonizing the area. The settlement that he had envisioned was to be called the Margravate of Azilia and organized in symmetrical departments, each separately secured against attack, so that the whole would be what he termed "one continued fortress." In other words, it would have been, as Frederica was intended to be, a barrier against the French on the Mississippi and the Spaniards in Florida, though Montgomery said little about this aspect because he wished to attract investors. His design fizzled out, but it is possible to discern in its conception some of the elements that characterized the thinking behind the settlement at Frederica.

FOUNDATION

Oglethorpe, with a small exploratory party, had landed on St. Simons Island in January 1734. He concluded that it was a good place for a military outpost, and when he returned to England later that year he persuaded his fellow Trustees of this. It was decided that the first settlers should be chiefly Salzburgers (persecuted Protestants emigrating from Germany), and Scottish Highlanders, persons more carefully selected than their Georgia predecessors for their trustworthiness, industry, and general suitability to the exacting conditions of an exposed, frontier position. A group of forty families, some Scots, some Germans, some English—about 230 persons—only a little more than a third of whom were men, sailed from England in October 1735. After a long and tempestuous voyage across the Atlantic, they anchored off Cockspur Island in the mouth of the Savannah early in February 1736.

The Salzburgers now displayed a reluctance to move on to Frederica, pleading that warfare was against their religion and that they preferred not to be placed in a position where fighting might be unavoidable. Most of them went to Ebenezer, where

there was already a thriving community of their own people, but a small number under Christian Adolph von Hermsdorf agreed to accompany Oglethorpe on his journey to the south.

The pioneers, with firearms, ammunition, tools, and supplies, set sail from Savannah on the morning of 16 February 1736 and reached St. Simons Island early on the 18th. The stores and equipment were landed, a few booths of palmetto thatch and poles were erected, and the evening was passed in jollification and the consumption of game brought in by the Indians. The families of these pioneers arrived at the island in March, having completed the voyage from Savannah with a celerity stimulated by consigning the stocks of strong beer to one boat only, so that those who fell behind forfeited their ration when it was distributed at nightfall. By the middle of March there were 44 men and 72 women and children at Frederica.

The settlement developed rapidly under Oglethorpe's personal daily supervision. The original plan of the town was described

later by Francis Moore, the first storekeeper: "Each freeholder had sixty foot in front, by ninety foot in depth, upon the high street, for their house and garden; but those which fronted the river had but thirty foot in front by sixty foot in depth. Each family had a bower of palmetto leaves, finished upon the back street in their own lands; the side towards the front street was set out for their houses." The palmetto bowers, according to Moore, gave the settlement the appearance of a camp, but they were tight in even the hardest rains and gave the inhabitants good shelter. The soil was hoed, and potatoes, maize, flax, hemp, barley, turnips, and pumpkins were planted in the hope of securing a crop the following year.

After 1739 the town was entered by either of two gates: the land port on the east side or the water port on the west. Broad Street, which passed through the land port and continued into the country, was the dividing boundary between the two wards, the north and the south, into which the town was organized. An area of about thirty-five acres was laid out in eighty-four lots on which the settlers built their homes along regular, spacious streets lined with orange trees. The garden lots were about half a mile away on the north, east, and south of the town, and the fifty-acre grants that the settlers received were situated in various parts of the rest of the island. Near the town was a large meadow on which cattle were grazed. Two wells were dug to insure a supply of water.

In 1739, when a Spanish invasion seemed possible, Oglethorpe fortified the town because, he told the Trustees, he "could not think of leaving a number of good houses and Merch'ts goods and, which was more valuable, the Lives of Men, Women and Children in an open Town at the mercy of every Party, and the inhabitants obliged to fly to a Fort and leave their effects, or suffer with them." The town was enclosed with a fence of cedar stakes ten feet high, at the foot of which was a moat into which water sometimes flowed at very high tide.

On a high bank at the western side of the town, where the inland waterway (the Frederica River) turned sharply, Oglethorpe erected a fort which, from its strategic position, was able to command the river approaches to the town. He began marking out the fort on the morning of 19 February 1736, and under the direction of Hermsdorf, the Salzburger, and Samuel Augspourger, a Swiss engineer and surveyor, it was almost completed by the end of March. Oglethorpe believed, perhaps somewhat pretentiously, that he had modelled the fort on the work of Vauban, a distinguished French military engineer of the late seventeenth century commonly recognized as being, in Macaulay's words, "the father of the science of fortification."

The fort at Frederica was built in the form of a square, with two bastions on the land side, two on the river side, and a projecting spur work facing the river. Thick, timber platforms were laid on each bastion and on the spur for cannon, and under

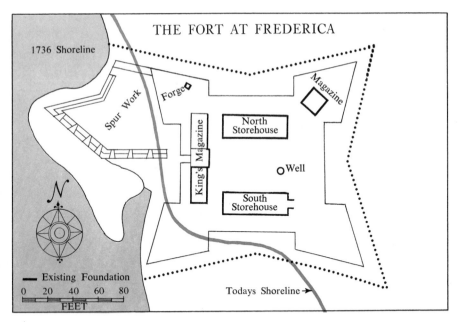

THE FORT AT FREDERICA

1736 Shoreline

Spur Work

Forge

Magazine

King's Magazine

North Storehouse

South Storehouse

Well

N

Existing Foundation

0   20   40   60   80
FEET

Todays Shoreline →

one bastion was a powder magazine. The outer walls were of earth lapped with tall cedar posts, at the base of which was a deep trench that served as a moat. Within the fort, the central area was used as a parade ground, at least one well was dug to supply water, and a large three-storeyed storehouse, a black-smith's forge, and a wheelwright's shop were constructed. The settlers who built the fort also manned it until 1738, when Oglethorpe's regiment arrived from England.

Also on St. Simons Island, a battery of cannon was set up a short distance south of Fort Frederica, and a small fort was built at the southern tip in order to command the entrance to Jekyll Sound. Huts were built to house the soldiers, and from a watch-tower the movement of vessels at sea could be observed and, if necessary, reported back to Frederica by horseman. Fort St. Simons, as it was called, was connected with the head-quarters at Frederica, nine miles away, by a very narrow road which the settlers cut through the marsh and thick woods of the middle and south-east of the island in little more than three days.

By 1740 Frederica had the appearance of a thriving settlement, and its population, including the soldiers, was perhaps approaching one thousand. It was a healthy settlement, and certainly the most attractive in Georgia at that time. The inhabitants in most cases were happy with it. The forests of live oak—an evergreen—festooned with grey moss, created a delightful scene then, as they do now. The blackish soil was regarded as fertile, the countryside abounded with game of various kinds, and the waters were replete with fish.

Nevertheless, Frederica was never able to lose the atmosphere of a frontier town whose principal business was defence. Each householder kept firearms in his home ready for use, military training took place each day, and discipline was strict. There was also an element of uncertainty about the town's future, for the financial support it received from the British Government and the Trustees was seldom sufficient for its needs, and in June 1736, when the annual parliamentary grant was drastically reduced for the ensuing year, the Trustees seriously considered transferring the settlers from St. Simons Island to Savannah. Oglethorpe, however, insisted on the settlement being retained as an essential item in the defence of the southern colonies. Writing in October 1738 to the Duke of Newcastle, the secretary of state in London, Oglethorpe admitted that Frederica had been expensive to establish and maintain, but, he argued, its military value would be great. After the declaration of war between Britain and Spain in 1739, he was able to prove the point.

ADMINISTRATION OF THE GEORGIA COLONY

The Trustees withheld powers of local government from the population of Georgia, and all regulations were made by the Trustees themselves meeting in London. For most of this period, Georgia lacked its own provincial assembly, there was no representative system, and no regular elections were held for any of the offices. The Trustees had resolved in 1732 that local administration in the colony should be by bailiffs, constables, and tithingmen, whose powers were largely of a judicial character, though no explicit instructions were ever sent them.

The administrative system organized in Savannah in 1733 was reproduced in Frederica in 1736. The Trustees appointed as bailiffs Thomas Hawkins, Samuel Perkins, and Edward Addison; as constables John Brooks and Samuel Davison; and as tithingmen William Allen and John Calwell. The settlers were granted their rights and privileges "according to the Law and Custom of the Realm of England," and the Trustees enjoined that there should be a town court in Frederica similar to that organized in Savannah, which decided all civil and criminal cases by grand and petty juries as in England. The court had the same

number of magistrates as the one in Savannah and possessed its own great seal, which Hawkins, the bailiff and surgeon, is said to have abstracted later and of which no trace has since been found. Justice was administered more efficiently and the court was conducted more successfully than in Savannah, not merely because of Oglethorpe's presence for long periods in Frederica but also because of the businesslike manner of the naval officer and searcher, Patrick Grant, who, according to Oglethorpe, was "a very brisk man."

Since Oglethorpe spent much of his time in Frederica, it was inevitable that he should have assumed a large measure of personal responsibility for the administration of the town and fort. He had been educated at Eton and Oxford and had seen military service in Eastern Europe under Prince Eugene of Savoy. In 1722 he had been elected to Parliament as a Tory, and it was in that capacity that he had acquired his interest both in philanthropic issues and in the colonization of Georgia. His influence on the shaping of policy towards the colony was immense, and the fact that he alone of the Trustees had been to Georgia moved the others at first to support his views. His decision to lead the first emigrants was due chiefly to his genuine, philanthropic enthusiasm for the colonization scheme, and partly, perhaps, to the removal of any domestic encumbrances when his aged mother died in June 1732.

The Trustees welcomed his decision and gave him liberal powers which he expanded rapidly as soon as he was across the Atlantic and beyond their immediate control. Since there was no governor nominated as such, and since the officials appointed by the Trustees were sometimes men who had been paupers or failures in England, it was natural for the people to look for leadership and guidance from Oglethorpe, decidedly a member of the upper classes and the personal representative of the Trustees.

In the main, Oglethorpe exercised his broad and undefined authority with justice and sense, and there is ample evidence of the respect which the settlers felt for him. On the other hand, he tended to be autocratic and puritanical, and his manner alienated some people. When Samuel Perkins, for example, found he could not earn a living in Frederica by tillage alone and decided to try his former trade of coach-making, Oglethorpe peremptorily forbade him to do so and threatened to burn the first chaise he made. It is not surprising to find Perkins complaining in 1741 of "such a number of Oppressions" that he was "incapable of bearing any more of them." Oglethorpe's increasing independence in the management of affairs eventually aroused apprehension among the Trustees, who in the late 1730s, grew wary of allowing him too much authority in civil matters.

In 1737 the Trustees appointed William Stephens as their secretary in the colony to keep them more regularly and circumstantially informed of affairs there. In 1741 Georgia was divided into two counties, Savannah in the north and Frederica in the south, separated by the Ogeechee River. Each county was to be under the jurisdiction of a president and a board of four assistants. Stephens became president of Savannah County, but no nomination was made to Frederica until Oglethorpe's wishes were known. It was expected that Oglethorpe himself would become president of Frederica County, but no appointment was ever made, and the local bailiffs remained in charge. In 1743, on Oglethorpe's final departure for England, the Trustees resolved that the bailiffs in Frederica should be subordinate to the Savannah president and assistants, to whom the recorder at Frederica was required to send frequent reports.

The various administrative officials in Frederica throughout these years were mostly effective and reliable in the discharge of their duties. The principal abuse, especially after Oglethorpe's departure, was the assumption by the military commander of a

THE HAWKINS-DAVISON HOUSE—*One of the better homes of Frederica, it was a row house of a type common in London after 1661.*

TYPICAL SMALL HOUSE—*Characteristic of the less affluent settlers, the cottage was reminiscent of English dwellings.*

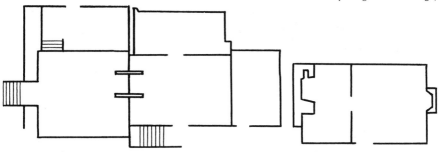

In the English basement to the left, Samuel Davison maintained his tavern. His mortared brick floor was of better construction than Dr. Hawkins' floor, which was laid on loose sand. Dr. Hawkins' use of his basement is unrecorded, but an English bayonet was found in the closet.

An ancient floor plan, even by Frederica standards, this "hall and parlor" house harks back to Medieval England. Such houses were built of wood, brick, or tabby.

measure of civil authority to which he was not strictly entitled, and there is some evidence to suggest that in the execution of justice the soldiers held an advantage over the civilian population. From the 1750's onward, the bailiffs, constables, tithing-men, and conservators of the peace were joined by increasing numbers of tax assessors, collectors, and inspectors, and other officials. Together they maintained a haphazard and sometimes eventful, but not necessarily inefficient, civil administration.

INDIANS

Vital to the success of the settlement at Frederica was the friendship of the Indians, whom Oglethorpe and the Trustees took care should be reconciled to British intrusion on their lands, their co-operation gained in trading activities, and, if possible, their alliance won against the French and Spaniards.

Soon after the landing of the first settlers in Georgia in 1733, Oglethorpe negotiated a treaty with representatives of a branch of the neighbouring tribes of the Creek nation. The Creeks agreed to allow the colonists to trade in their towns, and they ceded all lands in the tidewater region that they themselves did not require, retaining only the islands of Ossabaw, Sapelo, and St. Catherines for bathing, hunting, and fishing. The Indians also agreed to have no more communication with the French or Spaniards, and promised to observe the treaty for "as long as the sun shall shine or the waters run into the rivers." This resulted in the pacification of all the tribes of the Lower Creek nation and enabled the colony to be extended down the coast, thus opening the way for the establishment of Frederica.

This friendly relationship was stabilized in 1734 by the visit to England of Tomochichi and other chieftains of the small group of the Creek nation living on the south bank of the Savannah who had made the treaty. Tomochichi was about ninety years old, and his wife was described as "an old ugly creature," but Tooanahowi, the grand-nephew, later fighting ally of Oglethorpe on St. Simons Island, was then a handsome youth of fifteen and the object of Queen Caroline's affectionate attention while in London. The visit of the Indians to England helped not only to cement the treaty relationship but also to arouse interest in the Georgia project at a time when public support was needed for establishing a new settlement at Frederica.

The climax of Anglo-Indian friendship in Georgia during this crucial period was a ten-day conference in August 1739 at Coweta, the principal town of the Lower Creeks and situated well inland on the Chattahoochee. Accompanied by a few soldiers and servants, Oglethorpe journeyed nearly three hundred miles through a wilderness of morasses, thickets, and forests of pine to attend a council of the tribes. Amid splendour, luxury, and feasting, he negotiated an agreement which, among other things, confirmed the colonists in the ownership of their lands. The outcome of the conference was a triumph for Oglethorpe, a sick man at the time. He succeeded in confirming the understanding with the Indians at a critical juncture, for Britain and Spain were on the verge of war, and France was watching for an opportunity to embarrass its rivals in the New World. Christian Priber, for instance, was operating among the Cherokees as a French agent, and having donned Indian dress, learnt Indian language, and adopted Indian ways of life, was winning some influence when he was captured by British traders and immured in the barracks at Frederica until he fell ill and died.

At Coweta in August 1739, Oglethorpe had accomplished the important task of preventing significant sections of the neighbouring Indians from being turned against the British colonies by Spanish and French influence. It was an achievement of some consequence, for when he returned from Coweta to Frederica he learnt that Britain and Spain were at war.

ATTACK

On the formal declaration of hostilities between Britain and Spain in October 1739, Oglethorpe was instructed by the British Government to attack St. Augustine. The resources at his command, though not generous, were adequate for the task. In June 1737 he was commissioned a permanent Captain of the Independent Company of Foot stationed on St. Simons Island and given the additional war-time commission of General and Commander in Chief of the Forces in South Carolina and Georgia. Little more than two months later he was commissioned permanent Colonel of the Regiment of Foot for the Defense of His Majesty's Plantations in America, and soon afterwards the regiment of six hundred men was ordered to Georgia. This organization, listed in the War Office records as the 42nd, but commonly known as Oglethorpe's Regiment, contained companies of the 25th Foot, then garrisoning Gibraltar and later known as the King's Own Scottish Borderers.

In May 1740, Oglethorpe raised an independent company of Highland foot, which gained the distinction of being the first unit of the British army serving in America to wear tartan. In 1743,

Oglethorpe's Regiment was augmented by the transfer from the Tower of London of about forty men from the Black Watch who had been punished for mutiny not by death but by sentence to serve in the colonies.

Oglethorpe, who had gone to England in 1737 to make arrangements for his regiment, had returned to St. Simons Island in 1738. He warned the people of Frederica that there was danger of a Spanish invasion and suggested that any who might be afraid should depart, but at this time all decided to remain. After war was declared, Oglethorpe responded to his instructions from London to attack the Spanish fortress at St. Augustine in Florida, and at the beginning of December 1739 a preliminary incursion was made to within a few miles of it, primarily to test the enemy's strength and learn something about his preparations. The Spaniards refused an encounter, and the Georgia forces withdrew after inflicting a few casualties and destroying some horses and cattle.

In January 1740, Oglethorpe led a second expedition into Spanish territory, and within a few days reduced and captured

several small, crumbling, and lightly manned outlying Spanish forts. He then returned to the mouth of the St. Johns River, which was well inside Spanish territory, and there was joined by forces from South Carolina under Colonel Alexander Vanderdussen. With an army now of about 900 men, assisted by nearly a thousand Indians, Oglethorpe began his march into Spanish territory in earnest, and at day break of 15 June reached the abandoned Spanish outposts on the north side of St. Augustine.

A plan to capture the city by storm, involving a combined operation by land and naval forces, was thwarted by Spanish half-galleys moored in the channel between Anastasia Island and the castle. The water being too shallow to permit the British men-of-war near enough to dislodge them, the only alternative was to change the plan of campaign and resort to a siege in the hope of starving out the garrison. For this purpose, a party of 140 men under Colonel Palmer was detached to Fort Moosa (*Mose,* in Spanish), two miles from St. Augustine, with orders to intercept all supplies coming to the city from the interior. The commander of the naval squadron stationed one of his ships to guard the passage to the castle by way of Matanzas Inlet, and employed the remainder in blockading the mouth of the harbour, so that the Spaniards were cut off from all supplies by sea.

Oglethorpe's summons to the Spanish governor to surrender was met with mocking scorn, and thereupon the British general directed his guns to open up. This was answered by an equally spirited fire from both the fort and the half-galleys in the harbour, and some warm fighting took place between the Spanish flotilla and the blockading naval squadron. The cannonade was maintained briskly by both sides for nearly three weeks, but with little effect.

In the meantime, a detachment of 300 Spaniards made a sortie on the night of 25 June, and at sunrise the next morning, after desperate hand-to-hand combat, captured Fort Moosa, taking over 30 prisoners and killing nearly 70 of the garrison, including Colonel Palmer. This victory heartened the Spanish garrison. Small Spanish vessels eluded the British ships guarding the Matanzas Inlet, a secondary access to the harbour, and brought provisions to St. Augustine. All hope of forcing the city to surrender now disappeared, and the besieging forces became disheartened. The heat of the summer sun was intense, the troops were weary, and some of the South Carolinians decamped. By 20 July, when supplies were short and the hurricane season was approaching, the siege had been abandoned.

Its failure can be attributed partly to inadequate support from Britain and the other colonies. This must be qualified, however, by surveying the campaign in the wider setting of the whole war. To the British Government, the reduction of St. Augustine was not a task of high priority. Spain's empire in the Caribbean was a glitteringly attractive prey, but it was essential to be selective, for Britain's national resources were not unlimited. A more lucrative prize was Cuba, the pearl of the

Antilles, or Cartagena, the strongest port in Spanish America, destruction of which would deal a crippling blow to the enemy's whole position in the New World.

Nor could the colonies themselves, other than Georgia and South Carolina, be expected to exhibit much interest in what was, even to them, a comparatively remote Spanish outpost. The capture of St. Augustine would benefit all the colonies, but it was situated in good defensive country and begirt with an almost impenetrable morass. The hot season was commencing; insects, sand-flies, and mosquitoes were prevalent, and inland there would be danger of fever. The American colonies did not have a good record of mutual military assistance, and, except for South Carolina and Georgia, the little war on the southern frontier was not such as to stimulate particular concern. The other colonies had already provided troops for a Caribbean expedition. Now they cast an approving, well-wishing eye on Oglethorpe's expedition, but they did not feel any urgency about the campaign and they had little incentive to raise additional troops to serve among the thickets, glades, swamps, and sand dunes of northern Florida.

South Carolina was the exception in that it gave Oglethorpe substantial assistance. Although that colony was also charged with the defence of the southern frontier, the troops it sent failed to co-operate well with the rest of Oglethorpe's forces and some of the volunteers, it was said, "made more haste to return home than was for their credit." Their commander, Colonel Vanderdussen, condemned "the dastardly behaviour" of the volunteers and admitted that some of his officers had not conducted themselves as they should. However, as was to be expected, perhaps, the South Carolina Assembly rejected the charge that South Carolina was "in the least degree the cause of the ill-success of the expedition," and exonerated the troops who had served in it.

Even if there had been prompt support from Britain and the other colonies, it is doubtful whether the result would have been different. It is true that the Spaniards in St. Augustine were hard-pressed for a time and suffered severe privation, but the outcome of the siege illustrated the strength of the Spanish position and the relatively heavy price the attackers would have been obliged to pay in order to capture it. The Spanish regular troops, the militia, the convicts, and the free Negroes, all conducted themselves with courage and steadiness throughout the siege; few deserted. Although the Spanish commander was prevented from making an immediate counter-attack because of the weakness of his forces, he confessed that they were but little weaker than those commanded by Oglethorpe.

Some historians have charged Oglethorpe with indecision during the campaign, illustrated by his rushing back and forth between St. Augustine and the St. Johns River, tiring both himself and his men, and, according to Edward McCrady, an historian of South Carolina, showing himself to be "lacking in all the qualities necessary for an independent commander." This is a harsh view of the general's conduct. It is not always pointless to rush back to base to ensure that essential supplies have arrived. Moreover, success was dependent upon speed, and the inability of the South Carolina troops to join him earlier in the expedition resulted in the campaign being conducted in the hot season, and this rendered protracted operations impossible.

At dawn, 20 July 1740, the Spanish garrison realized the British were gone. Oglethorpe—tired, disappointed, and sick with fever—took his dispirited army back to Frederica, but in good order "with drums beating and colours flying." He had failed to take St. Augustine, but he had succeeded at least in delaying Spanish preparations to attack Georgia, and his policy now was obviously to strengthen the colony's defences against the expected Spanish invasion.

DEFENCE

In April and May 1741 Oglethorpe wrote to both the prime minister and the secretary of state in London that the security of all the southern colonies depended on the preservation of Georgia, and that reinforcements were needed urgently. During the succeeding months he repeatedly appealed to the British Government for more cannon to defend Frederica and for money, troops, and supplies to strengthen his forces, which he considered inadequate for the responsibilities that would be imposed on them. The British Government, however, would not provide substantial reinforcements for Georgia, which it regarded as an area of secondary importance to operations in Europe and the Caribbean. By June 1742, when the Spanish attack on Georgia was imminent, Oglethorpe was still being left to his own initiative. The defences were unsound, he wrote from Frederica, "being weak in cannon and shot, never having had any from England, nor indeed anything else since my last arrival in this country, but one store ship with powder and small-arms. . . ." It was too late, he told the Duke of Newcastle, to ask again for reinforcements, as the issue would be decided before they arrived: "I hope," he said, "I shall behave as well as one with so few men and so little artillery can."

The southern colonies in 1742 were fortunate in having a man of Oglethorpe's calibre to command their defence. He was not an imaginative or particularly forceful commander, but he was brave, proud, and generally popular. Throughout June 1742 he took such precautions as he could, and by the time the Spanish ships were first sighted, in early July, preparations for their reception were well advanced. He called in the rangers from their various posts, brought down the Highland company from Darien, and successfully appealed to his Indian allies, among whom was Tooanahowi, the heir of Tomochichi.

The invading forces were commanded by Manuel de Montiano, who had been the governor of Spanish Florida since 1737. Montiano's instructions were to seize St. Simons Island, move northward along the coast, destroying plantations and settlements, and then persuade Negro slaves in South Carolina to join the invader, promising them land and freedom. Estimates vary widely as to the size of the force he had at his disposal, but he had assembled approximately 3,000 men, including a number of armed Negroes, and had the support of a large fleet of men-of-war and small transport vessels. His initial plan was to surround St. Simons Island, sever Oglethorpe's lines of supply and communication, and land the bulk of the invading force on the beaches in the south of the island.

On Monday, 16 July, a strong east wind and a favourable flood tide brought the Spanish fleet into Jekyll Sound, and, having weathered the fire from the guns at Fort St. Simons covering the narrow inlet to the sound, it continued to the west side of the island and anchored opposite Gascoigne Bluff, named after James Gascoigne, the naval captain of the vessels stationed at Frederica, who had his home and plantation there. The Spaniards disembarked on the bluff a little below Gascoigne's plantation, and the next day marched south to take possession of the abandoned Fort St. Simons, making it their headquarters. Oglethorpe had spiked most of his guns at Fort St. Simons, not very efficiently according to the Spanish account, and withdrawn his forces to Frederica.

Montiano was encouraged by his early success and began planning an attack on Frederica itself. For this purpose, he sent out patrols to reconnoitre and test the outlying defences of the town. On the morning of Wednesday, 18 July, nearly 200 Spaniards and Indians marched up the road to within a mile and a half of Frederica. On learning of the Spanish approach, Oglethorpe ordered the regiment to move down the road. Then, leaping upon the first horse that came to hand, he led a force of Rangers, Indians, and the Highland Independent Company— the fastest-moving troops he had—to attack the enemy force in the defiles of the woods before it could deploy in the open ground near Frederica. An immediate assault routed the enemy, Oglethorpe himself taking two prisoners. He pursued the remnant as far as an open meadow, and concealed the troops, along with three platoons of the regiment that had joined him, in the woods at the edge of the field. He then returned to Frederica to order out his Marine Boatmen and the rest of the Rangers.

While at Frederica, he heard firing. Hurrying back toward the front, he met some of his men retreating in disorder. They told him that they had been routed by another Spanish force and that Lieutenant Sutherland, among others, was killed. A rain shower, which could render their muskets useless, perhaps excused their withdrawal, but Oglethorpe ordered the officers to rally their men and return to the fight. Still hearing shots, he concluded that his men "could not be quite beaten," and spurred his horse toward the sound of battle. Arriving there he found Sutherland alive, well, and elated. Sutherland's platoon of the regiment and Lieutenant Mackay's Highland Company, had

stood fast and routed the enemy with well placed fire. The two lieutenants had prisoners to show for their efforts, including officers. A number of Spanish dead, some of them the famed Grenadiers, lay before the position.

As the rest of the regiment joined Oglethorpe, he moved his force down to a bridge nearer Fort St. Simons to cover it and prevent Spanish survivors from making their way back to their lines. He remained at the bridge until the next morning, when he marched his men back to Frederica.

Sutherland's and Mackay's engagement won for them mention in dispatches and, for Sutherland, promotion to Brigade Major. As years passed, both men won fame as the victors of the Battle of the Bloody Marsh. The battle, small as it was in terms of modern warfare, caused considerable stir in America and in England. Eagerly, then and later, people sought details, details that were forthcoming in magazines and later accounts.

One such relation, heard decades after the battle from British survivors, would have us believe that the Spaniards marched

into a trap: assuming the contest to be over for the day, they obligingly stacked arms and sat down to take refreshment. From out of the brushwood rose a Highland bonnet on a stick, the pre-arranged signal for the British to pour volley after volley into the recumbent enemy until the ground was strewn with dead and dying. When the English and Highlanders rushed out with bayonets leveled and broadswords flashing, the remaining Spaniards fled in all directions, some into impassable marshes, some into impenetrable thickets, some through a defile into the tomahawks of approaching Indians, and only a few to the safety afforded by the guns of their battery and ships near Fort St. Simons.

This later account probably confused the fighting of 18 July with some skirmishing that took place a few days subsequently. Then, a party of Rangers and Indians crept to within musket distance of the Spanish camp and shot a number of enemy soldiers who indeed were dining. But however the fight took place, and Oglethorpe's terse account does not give romantic details, it is certain that English discipline and Scottish dash stopped a column of Spain's better troops.

After this victory, the Battle of Bloody Marsh as it came to be called, because, it was said, the marsh was red with the blood of the wounded and dead, Oglethorpe concentrated on strengthening the defences of Frederica. On learning, however, from an escaped prisoner that there was dissension among the invaders, and that they had encamped in separate places, he decided to launch a surprise attack in the night. He left Frederica on the afternoon of Monday, 23 July, and with a force of 500 men marched to within two miles of the main enemy camp, halting there in order that he might reconnoitre the ground. The attempt to surprise the invader was now frustrated by the desertion of a Frenchman who had joined the British as a volunteer. Oglethorpe, realizing that with his intentions known to the enemy an attack would be futile, had to abandon the idea.

Nevertheless, by paying a Spanish prisoner to deliver a misleading letter to the Frenchman, Oglethorpe tried to use the deserter as a channel to convey to the Spanish commander the impression that the British forces were much stronger than had been supposed. The Spaniards were not easily deceived and were inclined to treat the information they acquired through the deserter with considerable caution, but Oglethorpe's stratagem was providentially assisted on 24 July by the appearance out at sea of five vessels, part of a small naval force sent by the Governor of South Carolina to watch the movements of the enemy. This seemed to authenticate the information secured through the deserter, and the Spaniards, according to the journal kept on the expedition by the Marquis of Casinas, fearing "not so much what was involved, nor the vessels in sight, as the vessels which might follow in greater force," resolved to abandon the invasion and begin re-embarking their troops at once. This they did, after burning the barracks and officers' houses at Fort St. Simons, but with such precipitation that they left behind their guns, ammunition, provisions, and unburied bodies.

The campaign was heralded in America as an important victory over Spanish arms. It was believed that had the enemy been successful in the attack on Frederica, he would have moved speedily against the more northerly strongholds. The action was, indeed, a triumph for Oglethorpe, although he was not personally involved in the battle at Bloody Marsh. It might have been a greater triumph if the ships from South Carolina had acted with promptness, for Oglethorpe hoped that their arrival would pen the Spanish vessels in Jekyll Sound and ultimately deliver them into his hands. But the South Carolina commanders were confident that the enemy would have difficulty in making headway on St. Simons, and therefore did not hurry to dispatch their ships. As Oglethorpe bitterly expressed it in a letter to the Duke of Montagu: "The men-o'-war acted by precedent of former times, and consequently did not come till all was over, and the Spaniards had full time to go off by sea."

Even so, the victory was a substantial one. Several colonies sent Oglethorpe letters of gratitude, and in February 1743 the King promoted him to permanent brigadier-general for his services in repulsing the Spaniards. It could well be argued that the repulse of the invasion was due more to Spanish mismanagement than to British skill and bravery, but it is a fair assumption that the Battle of Bloody Marsh saved the southern colonies from what might have developed into a serious situation threatening their very existence.

STALEMATE

Despite the victory of 1742, settlers in Frederica felt that the Spanish danger remained as real as ever. Many believed that the Spaniards, with the secret support of the French, were planning a strong push against the southern colonies, and in February 1743 Oglethorpe sent Captain Dunbar to London to seek assistance, "which if we have not," he said, "we must certainly perish." In the existing situation, he wrote, "I shall do the best I can, but have reason to apprehend the worst of consequences from the great numbers of the enemy if I have not timely support." The British Government was not convinced, however, and Oglethorpe was ordered to reduce his military expenditure as much as possible. He continued to apply for supplies and reinforcements, but without effect, until, his patience exhausted, he disclaimed any responsibility for what might happen as a result of the British Government's attitude.

In fact, the British Government could not afford to lavish money or troops on what was undeniably a minor aspect of the war. France was moving into alliance with Spain, and the tremendous range over which hostilities would soon be conducted, and the important commitments Britain had all over the globe, made it inevitable that the plight of Georgia should have scant attention paid to it. The British Government had to dispose its forces with care: it had obligations in Hanover; it was bound to give support to Austria and Savoy; it had to provide for a struggle with France that would stretch from the sunny waters of the Indian Ocean to the rugged backwaters of North America; and it had to beware lest Gibraltar and the Mediterranean fell under Bourbon domination.

Nevertheless, Oglethorpe was not content to remain inactive. Firmly believing that the Spaniards would return to the attack, he decided to draw them into battle before they were reinforced from Havana. Accompanied by a number of Indians, a detachment of Highlanders, and a part of his regiment, Oglethorpe landed in Florida on the night of Wednesday, 20 March 1743, and frightened the enemy into the lines of St. Augustine. Convinced that the city was too strong to take by storm, he endeavoured to lure the Spaniards into ambush by hiding most of his army from sight and parading a small force outside the lines. The ruse was unsuccessful, the enemy declining to leave the fortifications, and the attackers were obliged to return to Frederica, having marched nearly a hundred miles in four days. Thus ended the general's last expedition against the Spaniards, and a few months later he sailed finally to England.

Thereafter, the southern frontier with the Spanish settlements was relatively quiet. Discussions about peace began in 1745, and in 1748 a treaty was signed leaving the real causes of dispute much as they had been before the war. Nothing was said about the boundaries of Georgia and Florida, and, indeed, so far as America was concerned the war had decided nothing. A new and important fact had been revealed, however. This was that France, not Spain, was now the main danger to Georgia and the other colonies. Henceforward, defence was directed not against the Spaniards in Florida but against the French and their Indian allies moving in from the region of the Mississippi. This change proved to be a decisive factor in the future of Frederica.

PEOPLE

Many of the sites of the homes in Frederica, and the names of their occupants, are known to us and have been clearly marked on the ground. A selection of names indicates the range of trades that were represented in what was always a very small community. John Calwell, the tallow chandler, was also a tithingman and bailiff, and in 1743 served as an engineer with the troops. George Spencer was a bricklayer, though erecting fences was his main occupation in Frederica. Daniel Cannon was carpenter, builder, and farmer, but like several other inhabitants he left for South Carolina in the early 1740's. William Abbott was a woodcutter, and after 1749 was in charge of the storehouse. John Levalley was a shoemaker and Donald Griffith was a cordwainer, but they both left the town after a comparatively short stay. William Allen was a baker and tithingman, but in 1741 he, too, went to South Carolina. Richard Lawley sold ironware; Mrs. Elizabeth Harrison received five pounds a year for officiating as midwife; William Forrester received twelve pence a day as postman making daily trips between Frederica and Fort St. Simons. The list of names could be extended to include practically every trade that a pioneer, frontier community needed. Clearly, the Trustees had chosen the Frederica settlers with great care.

Several of the more important persons in the community had

their homes outside the town. Oglethorpe's home was on a 300-acre tract to the south-east of the town at a point where the road entered a wood. It was commonly referred to as the Farm, and consisted not only of a cottage shaded from the sun by the foliage of huge, overhanging live oaks, but also of a delightful garden and an orchard of grapes, figs, and oranges; to the westward, across the meadow, the town and fort were in full view. A large stone tablet now marks the presumed site of Oglethorpe's home.

In 1771 the cottage was granted to James Spalding, a Scotsman who had come to Georgia eight years before and whose extensive commercial activities were considered by William Bartram, the Philadelphia naturalist, who visited him in 1773, as having contributed significantly toward the restoration of Frederica's economic importance. In 1772 Spalding married Margery, the daughter of William McIntosh and niece of Lachlan McIntosh. Spalding's son, Thomas, born in 1774, became an early historian of the area and a prominent agricultural writer. He lived not only on St. Simons Island, but also on nearby Sapelo. Upon his death, at a venerable age in the middle of the nineteenth century, he was buried at St. Andrews Church, Darien, the home parish of the Scottish settlers who fought so well for Georgia.

Captain Gascoigne, the naval officer, possessed a house and plantation near the station where his ship rode, and in addition to several out-houses seems to have also managed a storehouse for supplies and a careening ground for the repair of ships. Captain George Dunbar, a Scotsman of good family and educational background, who commanded a ship that plied between Georgia and England with passengers and cargo until he settled in Frederica in 1741, possessed a substantial plantation on the bank of a creek named after him.

Captain Raymond Demere, a wealthy French Huguenot who

had served for ten years with the British army in Gibraltar and was one of the oldest officers in Oglethorpe's Regiment, lived in a homestead known as Harrington Hall, named after Lord Harrington, under whom Demere had served in Spain. It was enclosed entirely with orange trees and Christmas berry, and was situated about half a mile along a road that ran due east from Oglethorpe's cottage. In addition to Harrington Hall, no trace of which has remained, he owned a tract of land further south which later became known as Harrington, the name it bears today.

Demere was a close friend of Oglethorpe, who presented him with his desk when he left Georgia, and possessed a knowledge of the Spanish language that was useful during the war. After Oglethorpe's Regiment was disbanded in 1749, Demere commanded one of the Independent Companies of South Carolina to which responsibility for the defence of the southern colonies was entrusted. He was at first stationed at Charleston, but in 1756 was sent into Cherokee country to build and garrison Fort Loudoun in the war that had broken out between the colonies and the French and Indians. In August 1757 he surrendered this command to his younger brother, Paul, and returned to Frederica to assume command of the fifty troops still stationed there, but in 1761 he sold his commission and passed the command at Frederica to Captain John Gray. Demere died in 1766, leaving most of his estate between his son and nephew, but according to his will £80 went to Betsy Demere: "The porre little girl," he declared, "She is not my daughter but as she was born under my Roffe I was always willing for to do something for her so that I would not have her to be called a Bastard."

The inhabitants of Frederica seem to have been generally more industrious and less discontented than those of Savannah, which gained a reputation for idleness and profligacy, but it is inevitable that in the records and reports that have come down to us the disorderly persons and the unusual occurrences should achieve a prominence that distorts the true nature and quality of the community. The normal, decent, quiet people who make up the majority of a village community such as Frederica, live their lives through and pass on unnoticed, seldom leaving anything more than birth, marriage, death, and land entries in the registries and historical records. This must be borne in mind if the following limited selection of brief profiles contains some persons of apparently less than exemplary character: they were present at Frederica in its early years, they were important in their own way to its development and daily life, but they were not necessarily typical of the town's population as a whole.

Francis Moore, storekeeper and recorder, warrants mention as the author of a description of life in Georgia that is among the most informative and reliable of contemporary accounts for the historian's purpose. He had served on the Gambia River as a writer for the Royal African Company, the principal English trading company involved in the traffic of Negro slaves from West Africa to the West Indies. He had journeyed inland in Africa making careful observations and drawings, and, as his publications on his travels in Africa and Georgia show, he brought a keen, perceptive mind and a facile pen to his work in Frederica. He and his wife were assigned Lot 20 in North Ward, where they appear to have erected both a brick and a wooden house. Moore was energetic and imaginative and served Frederica well, though the Trustees in London came to regard him as vain and dangerous when he questioned aspects of their policy. His appointment as recorder was eventually revoked, and in 1743 he returned to England to publish his travels under the title of "A Voyage to Georgia begun in the Year 1735." (This can be read in Volume I of the *Collections of the Georgia Historical Society.*)

Moore's successor as recorder was John Terry, who was of French extraction and possessed a useful knowledge of the French language. In addition to his post as recorder, he became a bailiff in place of Thomas Hawkins and worked as a silversmith, though under some disability, since the army officers, whom he annoyed by his carping criticism, sometimes prevented people buying from him. He sought refuge in Charleston when the Spaniards invaded St. Simons Island in 1742, but returned when the danger had passed and held a number of administrative offices that made him a man of considerable standing. He owned a plantation on Dunbar Creek, where he built himself a fine home and planted large numbers of orange trees which provided the place with the name Orange Grove. Terry was constantly in trouble while at Frederica, however, most of it of his own making. His complaints were legion—about the high price of food, about the scarcity of labour, about the low standard of morality, about the widespread dishonesty, and about the behaviour of the civil and military officers. He was suspended as recorder in Frederica but was offered a comparable position in Savannah that he took in 1745, to be met there with a charge of rape against his maidservant in Frederica. This was somewhat rich, in view of his previous strictures on other people's morality, or lack of it, but he was acquitted when the maidservant confessed that she had been encouraged to bring a false accusation against him. Terry ended his days in Charleston.

There is much documented gossip about Dr. Thomas Hawkins and his wife, Beatre. Hawkins was both apothecary and surgeon, terms which in the eighteenth century were employed broadly and liberally, and it was possible to qualify for both professions in what nowadays would be regarded as an extraordinarily short time. Hawkins occupied a brick house in Frederica and managed a 500-acre farm at a place still known as Hawkins Island. He was provided by the Trustees with medical materials and an allowance for a boat so that he could treat the sick in neighbouring parts of the colony, but he was disliked by his patients and seems to have been more interested in money than medicine: certainly, he was more attentive to those with the means to pay than to those without it. He quarrelled frequently with the other settlers, especially with the Davisons, his neighbours, and John Calwell accused him of removing the great seal from Frederica. Hawkins crossed Oglethorpe by breaking the rule not to shoot on Sundays, and in 1742 he was dismissed from the office of first bailiff. Mrs. Hawkins was a veritable shrew, a mean and neurotic troublemaker, whose temperament may be deduced from the fact that she beat her servant, broke a bottle over a constable's head, and threatened John Wesley with a pistol, biting him in the wrist when he attempted to disarm her.

Mrs. Hawkins found an ally for her machinations in Mrs. Welch, who was described variously as both a pretty woman and, by Charles Wesley, as "That poor blockhead." There has been a tendency to assume, on extremely slender evidence, that her morals were not of a high order. Her husband, John Welch, a carpenter and brewer, is thought to have been lazy, for he failed to improve his land significantly, although his house was among the better ones in the town.

Samuel Davison, a constable, kept a tavern, the bar of which was on the lower floor of his house. He and his wife, two daughters, and infant son were popular figures in the town and respected by the Wesleys, but they complained of unneighbourly treatment from Dr. Hawkins, and, like the Welchs, they left Frederica after a few years.

Among the less controversial of Frederica's worthies was Peter Grant, who was in charge of parades, fought at Bloody Marsh, and spent the rest of his life on the island, dying there early in the nineteenth century at the age of eighty-four. Grant had several brothers, and his sister eventually owned the lot on which the Hawkins house had been built. Patrick Houstoun, an officer in Oglethorpe's Regiment, acquired a house in Frederica by his marriage to the sister of Captain Dunbar and in 1741 he became a conservator of the peace, in 1747 the regimental adjutant, and in 1748 the quartermaster. He may have been sympathetic towards the malcontents in Frederica, and he ultimately moved to Savannah and succeeded to the family baronetcy. A son was to become Governor of Georgia.

Samuel Augspourger (later modified to Auspourger), who had come to America from Switzerland, arrived in Frederica from South Carolina in 1736 to be appointed land surveyor and engineer at the fort on a salary of three shillings a day. He drew a large-scale map of the town for the Trustees, who were delighted with it, but Oglethorpe removed him from office and he retired to his plantation on Little St. Simons.

About two miles from Frederica, but important to it, was the German Village, established by those Salzburgers who had come to Georgia with Oglethorpe and, unlike their compatriots, had decided to accompany him to St. Simons Island rather than join the other Salzburg settlement at Ebenezer. The Salzburgers kept very much to themselves; they were reluctant to learn English, and they kept in close touch with their fellow countrymen at Ebenezer. In 1743 the Society for the Propagation of the Gospel sent over to be their pastor John Ulrich Driesler, who spoke no English but had been advised by the Trustees that if he learnt it he would be in a position to serve both the German and English communities in several capacities. Driesler duly added to his pastoral duties, becoming both schoolteacher and, just before he died, chaplain to Oglethorpe's Regiment. He was succeeded at the Village by Joachim Zubli, but when the regiment was disbanded in 1749 the Salzburgers, who had lived by planting and fishing and trading with the officers and settlers in the town, left the island.

WORSHIP

Perhaps the most dramatic aspect of community life in early Georgia concerned the Church. Anglican organization in America in the eighteenth century was of a most haphazard character, although the authority of the Bishop of London had been extended over all the colonies. The clergy were never large in number, and were frequently of poor calibre, sometimes including individuals unable to secure a parish at home. Consequently missionary activity was often neglected, not only among the Indians but also among the pioneers in the outlying settlements such as Frederica. After 1701 the Society for the Propagation of the Gospel had attempted to revive missionary zeal in the colonies, and although it lacked proper support from the Church of England it had succeeded in strengthening Anglicanism in America. It was instrumental in sending over a few ardent clergy of talent who were not deterred by the rough, and even dangerous, conditions, and it came to epitomize the missionary and philanthropic motives in British colonial policy. Among its experimental grounds was Georgia, whose early development, like that of so many of the other colonies, was originally intended to have significant religious overtones.

From the inception of the colony, the Trustees made careful provision for religious guidance, but were not concerned to foster the Church of England to the entire exclusion of other denominations. They granted 300 acres in trust at Frederica for the maintenance of a clergyman and schoolmaster, and for other religious uses, but they had a series of misfortunes in their choice of ministers.

With Oglethorpe in the founding days of Frederica were Benjamin Ingham and Charles Wesley. Ingham had strict ideas about the observance of the sabbath: "My chief business," he wrote, "was daily to visit the people, to take care of those that were sick, and to supply them with the best things we had. For a few days at the first," he added, "I had everybody's good word; but when they found I watched narrowly over them, and reproved them sharply for their faults, immediately the scene changed. Instead of blessing, came cursing, and my love and kindness were repaid with hatred and ill-will." Finding himself in increasing trouble, Ingham hastened back to Savannah and in February 1737 returned to England.

Charles Wesley and his brother John, the founders of Methodism, left behind in England their widowed and penniless mother in the grip of her creditors, and went to Georgia with the intention primarily of spreading Christianity among the Indians and only secondarily of performing pastoral duties among the colonists. In this, they were pursuing their father's early interest in the Georgia project. The inhabitants regarded them as Roman Catholics in disguise, and in Savannah the young John Wesley was regarded with suspicion, it being thought that he had been sent to Georgia by the Trustees for some clandestine purpose.

Charles Wesley had come to Georgia as secretary for Indian affairs and to do routine secretarial work for Oglethorpe. In March 1736 he went to Frederica, partly to escape the crushing discipline his brother had exercised on the voyage from England. Within three weeks he had established twice daily prayers and a weekly communion, to which the congregation was summoned, not by church bell, but by the beat of a drum. He was not popular, however, because he tried to impose puritanical restrictions on people already threatened with a dull life at Frederica. When Dr. Hawkins was apprehended for firing a gun on a Sunday, and, incidentally, while Charles Wesley was preaching, Wesley was unjustly credited with instigating the arrest—a particularly ill-timed one, since a woman suffered a miscarriage while the doctor was immobilized in gaol. Some of the womenfolk in the town intrigued against Charles Wesley, and Mrs. Hawkins and Mrs. Welch spread unseemly and fabricated rumours that helped to prejudice Oglethorpe against him. Wesley came to be regarded in the town as a mischief-maker; he was shunned by the people—even his laundrywoman refused to wash his linen—and on the first Sunday in April 1736 his congregation was reduced to two Presbyterians and a Baptist. He soon left for Savannah and decided to return to England.

Charles's brother, John, was of sterner metal, but he, too, found himself unwelcome in Frederica whenever he preached there. His first visit, soon after Charles's departure, was in May 1736, when he stayed a month. He returned at the end of July for about twelve weeks, and made his final visit in January 1737, when he stayed nearly three weeks. He succeeded in setting up a small library, but wrote that he found "So little either of the form or power of religion at Frederica" that he was glad to be away from it. Except for Mark Hird and his family, John Wesley made no friends in Frederica, and Mrs. Hawkins threatened to shoot him. One of his congregation told him that the people liked nothing he did and that they could not tell what religion he was: "We never heard of such a religion before," he complained; "we know not what to make of

it." Wesley preached several times in Frederica, but hostility toward him grew, and he ultimately left the town despairing of the spiritual future of its people. He ran into worse trouble in Savannah, and he slipped away to South Carolina one evening in December 1737 in the company of a constable, a tithingman, and a barber, reputed to be three of the most objectionable persons in Savannah. It was the end of a lamentable episode in Wesley's career, but his short term of duty in Georgia gave him his first experience of practical affairs. It was a salutary, if chastening, lesson in social diplomacy, and as such it undoubtedly influenced his later conduct and his methods in effecting radical changes in the religious life of England.

Both the Wesleys had been, perforce, largely open-air preachers, because there was no proper chapel or church in Frederica until 1740. The storehouse was the meeting-place for services in the early months until a house was used for the purpose, but in 1738 work began on a building designed to be sixty feet long, twenty feet wide, and having three storeys, one of which was to serve as a chapel. It was not completed until May 1740, so that all the ministers before then were obliged to conduct their services in makeshift surroundings.

The ill-luck of the Trustees in their choice of ministers did not end with the departure of the Wesleys. George Whitefield was appointed to Frederica in December 1737, and he first visited the town in August 1738, when he stayed five days and took his first service under a large tree. Though Whitefield had been appointed to Frederica, he spent most of his time in Savannah. He visited Frederica again in 1740, but his zeal carried him beyond his nominal office as Anglican incumbent in Frederica, so that he became more of a minister at large. He was popular, but shocked some of the more conservative inhabitants by indications of unorthodoxy, such as pleading for faith alone and inveighing against the modern clergy as "slothful shepherds, dumb dogs, etc., who led their people dreaming on in a carnal security to destruction." Whitefield's refusal to be confined to Frederica or Savannah and his wanderings through the other colonies on a series of preaching tours meant that he left his Georgia parishes neglected, but he helped to begin the period of religious revival known in America as the Great Awakening.

Whitefield's failure to stay in Frederica necessitated the transfer there in April 1739 of William Norris, who had been the minister in Savannah since October 1738. Norris had been a source of disquiet to the Trustees from the moment he reached Georgia, and their doubts about his suitability were strengthened when he moved to Frederica. He complained about conditions, and William Stephens recorded in September 1740 that Norris was "a little chagrined at the small Number he could get together at any Time to hear him" and at the lack of proper religious facilities. Whitefield criticized Norris's way of life and accused him of playing cards with ladies when he ought to have been saving souls. While esteemed by many people, Norris's bad relations with officials, coupled with rumours of his familiarity with the maidservant who cleaned his house, undermined his authority. The Trustees were convinced that he was leading an idle life and neglecting his duties, and he returned to England in 1740, still full of complaints, including one against the Trustees for not having paid him his salary. The Society for the Propagation of the Gospel, however, was unconvinced of Norris's culpability, considering him to have been ill-treated in Georgia, and it resolved to employ him again as a missionary in the first suitable vacancy that arose.

The selection of Thomas Bosomworth to be a minister in Georgia was also ill-starred. He had the advantage of having lived in Georgia before taking holy orders in Britain, but he had the drawback, from the Trustees' point of view, of a coolly independent frame of mind. He was instructed to reside in Savannah, but he preferred Frederica, where, he said, "the people had been too long as sheep without a shepherd and driven to and fro with every wind of doctrine." In the summer of 1744, however, he contracted a fever which made him so ill, he lamented, that he was scarcely able to put pen to paper in order to draw his salary. In 1745 he left for Savannah and ultimately England, where he decided to join the campaign against the Young Pretender in the north. The Trustees regarded this decision as tantamount to his resignation, and Bartholomew Zouberbuhler, a Swiss, was appointed his successor. At last the Trustees were rewarded with an active and conscientious minister, who performed valuable service at Frederica, Savannah, and Augusta and travelled the colony for twenty years until his death in 1766.

CONDITIONS

The Church and education were closely related in early Georgia, just as education in England had been generally within the province of the Church since medieval times. In America the relationship was more unsystematic, but the same connection had always been there. New England had an exceptionally good record in educational facilities, but elsewhere the majority of colleges were virtually training establishments for the clergy, and there was a tendency for wealthy planters to send their sons to school and university in Great Britain. The Trustees could not hope to organize in a new settlement an educational system of the standard of the older colonies. Progress was impeded by the great distances between settlements, the poor state of such roads as there were, the widespread illiteracy among the early settlers, and the need for children to help in the fields.

Schooling, therefore, was of a variable quality in Georgia, and was probably of an inferior standard at Frederica. At the beginning of 1744, Bosomworth remarked on the great need for a schoolmaster in Frederica, and the following year the Trustees appointed John Ulrich Driesler at a salary of ten pounds a year.

Driesler, according to William Stephens, was "a Person of a most unspotted Character, who is respected for his great Virtues even by men of the loosest lives." He was the pastor of the Salzburg congregation, and as schoolmaster he taught in both English and German, the books being supplied by the Society for the Propagation of the Gospel. In addition to teaching the children by day, Driesler also managed an evening class for adults who wished to improve their education—not the first, but certainly among the earliest of such classes to be formed in the colonies.

Schooling, however, was spasmodic and generally of a low standard in the colony, and at Frederica, or, indeed, anywhere along the exposed southern frontier, it was necessarily of a particularly inadequate character. Nevertheless, considering the means at the Trustees' disposal and the situation of the settlements, it cannot be said that Georgia compared unfavourably in education with some of the other colonies, which had a longer history and whose frontiers were more secure. It is certain that, without the active interest of the clergy and the Society for the Propagation of the Gospel, the standard would have been very much lower.

Frederica was a well-built town. Unlike Savannah, where buildings were predominantly of timber, those of Frederica were sometimes built of tabby—a concrete made of sand, water, and lime obtained from burning oyster shell, and an aggregate of shell that formed a soft and plastic substance when mixed but later hardened and became durable and difficult to destroy. The houses of some of the wealthy inhabitants were of brick brought over from England, and possessed window glass and sashes. Archaeological research in the 1950s confirmed and augmented our knowledge of the character of the homes in which the inhabitants of Frederica lived in the eighteenth century, and the precise sites of the houses of many known settlers were uncovered and marked. The most elaborate investigation was made on what had been the sites of two of the finest private homes in the town, that of Thomas Hawkins, doctor, apothecary, and bailiff, and that of Samuel Davison, constable and publican, which were adjoining with a party wall, although their families were never on good terms with each other. Excavation unearthed clay pipes, bottles, and other objects that verified the existence of a tavern on the Davison site, and medicine bottles, ointment jars, and other artifacts that were evidence of medical practise on the Hawkins site.

Except for the fact that it was a frontier and fortress town, with all the uncertainties and restrictions which that entailed, there is no reason to believe that life in Frederica was significantly different from life in the other settlements in Georgia. All the settlements at this time were small, primitive, and precarious, and the whole colony existed under a cloud of doubt about the future. In some respects, Frederica, being a frontier town subject to the disciplinary requirements of a military outpost, was more orderly and better administered than some of the other towns in the colony.

Frederica, in these early years, was not an unpleasant place in which to live, although, of course, it had its share of minor hazards and irritations. The sand-flies would occasionally raise the settlers from their beds in the middle of the night and would have to be smoked out if further sleep was desired. Persons who wished to bathe in the rivers were advised to do so early in the morning before the alligators stirred. The officers of the regiment had a penchant for duelling, and there were a few unnecessary deaths as a result. Moreover, if Frederica was more civilized and orderly than Savannah, it was still a comparatively perilous community for the law-abiding: burglary and robbery were daily occurrences and rape was common enough for it to be said that no woman was safe without protection.

The proximity of the Spanish danger meant that the people of Frederica spent much of their time in military training, which perhaps had a deleterious effect on economic and social activity. The harvest of 1738 was almost entirely lost largely because the men were doing military duty, and when drought coincided with crop failures the people were reduced at one stage to feeding on alligators. A few settlers were discouraged by failure, and some left. Nearly all felt that the policy of the Trustees put the whole province at an economic disadvantage compared with the other southern colonies.

The aspect of the Trustees' policy that attracted the strongest criticism was the prohibition on the employment of slave labour. In 1734 the Trustees had drawn up a law imposing a fine of £50 on anyone importing a Negro into Georgia. The settlers, however, soon felt the need for slaves to help clear the land, especially as there was a general shortage of servants. Oglethorpe wrote to the Trustees in 1742 that servants were essential at Frederica: "Labouring hands are much wanting," he reported, "and there are many who are able and willing to pay their Passage for them." The shortage of servants was never properly overcome, but in the 1740s the settlers successfully flouted the prohibition on the importation of slaves, one method being to hire Negroes from South Carolina whose owners would re-claim their property whenever an attempt was made to enforce the regulations. As time went on, the president and assistants in Savannah increasingly connived at the presence of Negroes in Georgia, and by the beginning of 1748 many inhabitants of St. Simons Island possessed slaves, Alexander Heron, an officer in the garrison at Frederica, not only owning several but declaring that he would protect and uphold any others that were introduced into the area. In May 1748 the president and assistants wrote to the Trustees that it was impossible effectively to prevent slaves being brought into Georgia, and that an attempt to enforce the prohibition would cause depopulation, and in 1750 the Trustees at last repealed the law of 1734. Although the Trustees finally had to yield to public demand for Negroes, the prohibition may have served a useful purpose. It is at least arguable that the colony, and especially Frederica, on account of its frontier location, would not have been so well able to stand against the Spanish danger if it had contained a large Negro population.

There was some economic progress at Frederica. Cotton was grown there very early; the soldiers' wives spun it, and in 1740 cotton stockings were produced. Oglethorpe, loyal to the Trustees' determination that the colony should produce silk, planted six thousand mulberry trees which he had purchased from along the Savannah River, and at the south end of the island was the aptly-named plantation, Mulberry Grove. Orange trees lined Frederica's Broad Street, and dates, limes, figs, peaches, plums, and pomegranates were grown in the orchards, producing enough fruit to supply the town and garrison. By 1747 both maize and wheat were being produced on several farms.

Frederica was a remarkably healthy settlement, and the garrison was virtually free of sickness. Davison, the constable, wrote in 1738 that the birth-rate was high, and that "women bear who in Europe were thought past their time." It was also beautifully situated in green and shaded surroundings which delighted most of the inhabitants and which still impress the visitor. With so much in its favour, it is surprising, therefore, that life at Frederica gradually disintegrated after the settlement's role against the Spaniards had been served.

DECLINE

The settlements on St. Simons Island began their misfortunes during the war with Spain. Before their re-embarkation in 1742, the invading Spaniards destroyed the buildings at the southern end of the island, leaving only a house that they had consecrated for a chapel. At Frederica, in March 1743 the town magazine mysteriously exploded, much to the alarm of the town's inhabitants, who suspected a vagabond "Irish Papist" to have been the culprit. The sense of despondency was growing in these years. By 1747 the German settlers were noticed to have become "prejudiced against the place" and were already leaving, and two years later it was estimated that about two-thirds of the freeholders who had been on the island in the early part of the decade had departed.

The fort, once regarded as Georgia's main bulwark against the Spaniards, was allowed to fall into decay when it became clear that there was unlikely to be any more warfare on the southern frontier. After the ending of the 1739-1748 war, Oglethorpe's Regiment was disbanded. The officers and men were offered land and other inducements to remain in Georgia, and about 150 men with their families decided to do so. A detachment from the Independent Companies of South Carolina was maintained at Frederica until 1764, after which the garrison was reduced to seven men from the Royal American Regiment of Foot (troops recruited in the colonies and commanded by officers from Britain and Continental Europe). Throughout these years, the fortifications were sadly neglected.

In August 1751 the goods in the public storehouse at Frederica were taken to Savannah and put up for sale. In 1753 a visitor, with perhaps a touch of exaggeration, described the town as in a condition that reduced him to tears, "presenting the melancholy aspect of houses without inhabitants, barracks without soldiers, guns without carriages, and streets grown over with weeds." In 1755, when Governor John Reynolds toured southern Georgia, he found Frederica "in ruins, the fortifications entirely decayed and the houses falling down." Twenty old cannon were lying around spoilt by neglect, and other cannon originally mounted on the fort had been transferred to Savannah on the withdrawal of Oglethorpe's Regiment. It must be remembered, however, that the deplorable condition into which Frederica was permitted to fall was only one of several examples of the British Government's indifference to the defence of the frontiers in this period. All the forts along the Georgia borders were either dismantled or in ruins by 1755, and the only one effectively remaining was at Augusta, and even that was described as being so rotten that a great part of it was "propped up to prevent its falling."

Early in 1758 a fire destroyed much of what remained of the town at Frederica. In the early 1760s, parts of the fort were repaired under the vigorous direction of Captain John Gray, who assumed the command in 1761. In October 1762 he reported that he had installed some cannon with new carriages and platforms, surrounded the whole fort area with fascines and pickets covered with earth, and erected a parapet of bricks taken from the ruins of old houses. He asked the Governor of South Carolina for reinforcements, but was told that not one man more would be sent him and that he was to defend the fort "as you shall answer to the Contrary at your Peril, and if any Accident comes over your Post," the governor continued, "I shall make you Answerable for it," a threat which, as Gray remarked, was "a Sufficient peril of itself." Gray died a few days later, and although legislation in 1765 provided for the repair of the barracks, which were described as "in a ruinous condition," in 1767 the last detachment composing the depleted garrison was withdrawn.

St. Simons in general, as well as Frederica in particular, was experiencing misfortune. In 1756 the island was nearly submerged when the sea rose dramatically, a calamity repeated in 1804, 1824, 1854, 1898, and 1911, when fierce hurricanes left large areas of it under water. During the War of Independence, the island suffered at the hands of privateers and British soldiers. In November 1776, Captain William Oldis, a renegade from the province, came in an armed schooner with sixty men and pillaged the little settlements, eluding a party sent to apprehend them. On 10 August 1777 British forces landed on the island and captured a few Negroes and settlers, including Arthur Carney, who was a captain in the First Continental Battalion of Georgia Troops but, after his capture, espoused the royalist cause.

By the close of the War of Independence, little remained of Frederica, and although the legislature later tried to restore it, there was no response. In February 1796 special commissioners were named to lay out the town according to its original plan, open the streets, mark out the lots, and prepare a map, but the attempt to revive a semblance of the original town was a failure. Aaron Burr, Vice-President of the United States, who, after killing Alexander Hamilton in a duel, sailed secretly in

August 1804 to St. Simons Island to be the guest of his friend, Major Pierce Butler, was depressed by what he saw:

> Frederica, now known as Old Town, was about fifty years ago a very gay place, consisting perhaps of twenty-five or thirty houses. The walls of several of them still remain. Three or four families only now reside there. In the vicinity of the town several ruins were pointed out to me as having been formerly country seats of the Governor and officers of the garrison, and gentlemen of the town. At present nothing can be more gloomy than what was once Frederica. The few families now remaining, or rather residing there, for they are all new comers, have a sickly melancholy appearance, well assorted with the ruins which surround them.

On the other hand, J. Morse, another observer of Frederica at this time, calculated that the town had 72 inhabitants, and contemporary newspaper advertisements indicated that houses were still being built and sold there.

The tale of misfortune continued during the 1812-1814 war between Britain and the United States, a detachment of a hundred men from a British force on Cumberland Island capturing St. Simons and leaving three weeks later with 300 Negro slaves. By 1839 only three families resided at Frederica. The town was described by Frances Anne Kemble, an English actress, keen advocate of the abolition of slavery, and author of a diary of her residence on a Georgia plantation that later historians, notably Margaret Davis Cate, have pointed out contains a large number of serious errors. The diary remains an interesting source, and in it Frederica is depicted as "this curious wilderness of dismantled crumbling gray walls compassionately cloaked with a thousand profuse and graceful creepers." Writing on 17 April 1839, Mrs. Kemble remarked: "These heaps of rubbish and roses would have made the fortune of a sketcher; but I imagine the snakes have it all to themselves here, and are undisturbed by campstools, white umbrellas, and ejaculatory young ladies."

Mrs. Kemble had in mind a comparison with the ornate social life that was common elsewhere in Georgia and was not unknown on St. Simons. Indeed, a distinction needs to be drawn between the town, Frederica, and the island, St. Simons. For while the town was for most practical purposes already dead by the end of the eighteenth century, the island communities continued and, led by wealthy planters with refined tastes, often prospered. The island enjoyed a reputation as a summer resort. Georgia planters occasionally held regattas there, and in 1832 the St. Simons Island Agricultural and Sporting Club was formed. C. C. Jones, a nineteenth century historian of Georgia writing after the Civil War, was almost lyrical when trying to recapture the atmosphere of the island in earlier days:

A mean temperature of about fifty degrees in winter, and not above eighty-two degrees in summer, gardens adorned with choice flowers, and orchards enriched with plums, peaches, nectarines, figs, melons, pomegranates, dates, oranges and limes—forests rendered majestic by the live-oak, the pine, and the magnolia grandiflora, and redolent with the perfumes of the bay, the cedar and the myrtle,—the air fresh and buoyant with the South-East breezes, and vocal with the notes of songbirds,—the adjacent sea, sound, and inlets, replete with fishes,—the shell roads and broad beach affording every facility for driving and riding,—the woods and fields abounding with game in their season, and the culture and generous hospitality of the inhabitants, impressed all visitors with the delights of this favoured spot.

This, of course, was excessively rhapsodic, but it was not an untypical reaction to the island in the nineteenth century.

Frederica's decline, however, was never arrested. In 1861 troops were again stationed there and elsewhere on the island, guarding the entrance to Brunswick harbour, but with the close of the Civil War the history of Frederica may be said to have been brought to an end.

During the Civil War, some small skirmishes took place on the island. The lighthouse, built in 1808 on the site of Fort St. Simons, was destroyed by Confederate forces in 1862, but was re-built in 1871. Christ Church, which had been erected at the beginning of the century on land that had formerly been garden lots of the old town, was severely damaged by Federal forces during the Civil War, and an entirely new structure was begun in 1884.

The new church was built by the wealthy grandson of William E. Dodge, Anson Greene Phelps Dodge, Jr., in memory of his wife, whose body was buried in a vault under the chancel—a romantic piece of sea-island history that was to be popularized later in Eugenia Price's *The Beloved Invader.*

COMMEMORATION

At the end of the nineteenth century, there were still ruins to be seen at Frederica, and the tower of the barracks and the north wall of the fort were virtually intact. In 1903, the land on which the fort ruins were situated was given by Mrs. Belle Stevens Taylor to the Georgia Society of the Colonial Dames of America, which repaired and restored the ruins of the fort, but an attempt to restore the town for public interest failed for lack of adequate financial support. Within a few years, it became evident that the foundations were being undermined by the current of the river, and unsuccessful appeals were made to the state legislature for help in undertaking their proper preservation. In 1924, the War Department, after an investigation into the requirements and estimated cost of repairs, agreed to approve the necessary appropriation if the property were deeded to the Government. The Society of Colonial Dames consented to this, but there were legislative, technical, and financial complications, and no further progress was made at that time.

Nevertheless, the historical interest in Frederica was kept alive. In 1936, the bi-centenary of the town's foundation was

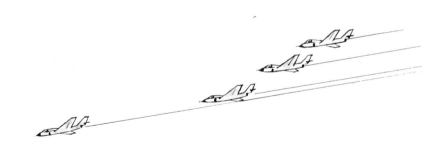

celebrated in the presentation of an historical pageant, and on 7 July 1942, the two hundredth anniversary of the Battle of Bloody Marsh was commemorated by a ceremony that concluded with the singing of verses both of "America" and of "God Save the King."

In June 1941 the Fort Frederica Association was formed, and, under the leadership of Judge and Mrs. S. Price Gilbert of Atlanta, Mrs. Margaret Davis Cate, and Alfred W. Jones of Sea Island, it succeeded in raising the financial support required to persuade the United States Government to purchase the lands on which the old fort and town were situated and protect them as a national monument. In September 1945 Fort Frederica National Monument was established under the aegis of the National Park Service of the U. S. Department of the Interior.

In this way, the memory is preserved of a colonial settlement that was important not only to Georgia but, in some measure, to all the Thirteen Colonies during the conflict with Spain between 1739 and 1748. Frederica's significance in the defence of the colonies against Spain in the 1740s has been exaggerated, perhaps, by some Georgia historians, especially by those writing in the nineteenth century, and to employ such classical comparisons as Thermopylae, as C. C. Jones liked to do, is to distort Frederica's role in the general context of an Anglo-Spanish war that was fought largely elsewhere and over a number of disputes, of which the Georgia boundary was only one.

Nevertheless, Frederica will always hold an honoured place in American history as the bastion upon which the security of Georgia and the southern colonies depended. Frederica has been a "dead town" for a long time, but its crucial role in the eighteenth century, and its contribution to the defence of the southern frontier, have their real and lasting memorial in the Georgia that survived those early difficult years to become one of the original States of the Union.

TREVOR R. REESE

Dr. Reese is Reader in Commonwealth Studies at the Institute of Commonwealth Studies, University of London. He was formerly Leverhulme Fellow in Commonwealth Studies at the University of Hull, England, Senior Lecturer in History at the University of Sydney, and Lecturer in History at Newcastle University, Australia. He was born in England and educated at King Edward's School, Birmingham, at the University of Sheffield, where he took a first class honours degree in modern history in 1952, and at the University of London, from which he received his doctorate in 1955. He is a Fellow of the Royal Historical Society and is the author of *Colonial Georgia: A Study in British Imperial Policy in the Eighteenth Century* (University of Georgia Press, 1963), of *Australia in the Twentieth Century: A Short Political History* (Praeger, New York, 1964), and of *The History of the Royal Commonwealth Society, 1868-1968* (Oxford University Press, 1968).

PETER SPIER

Peter Spier was born in Amsterdam, Holland, but grew up in Broek in Waterland which Americans know as the setting for *Hans Brinker and the Silver Skates*. Educated in Amsterdam, Mr. Spier attended the Rijksakademie voor Beeldende Kunsten. After overseas service with the Royal Netherlands Navy, he returned to civilian life and joined Elsevier's Weekblad, Holland's largest weekly, as a reporter in Paris. In 1952 he came to Houston, Texas, where Elsevier Publishing had a branch. But he soon moved to the New York area and began illustrating for magazines and publishers and doing his own books for children. His native Holland provided the setting for *The Cow Who Fell in the Canal* (Doubleday, 1956); *The Fox Went Out on a Chilly Night* (Doubleday, 1960) followed and was a runner-up for the Caldecott Medal. Mr. Spier's first book in the Mother Goose Library, *London Bridge is Falling Down!* won the Horn Book—Boston Globe award; *To Market, To Market!* set in historic New Castle, Delaware, was runner-up for the same award; newest in the Mother Goose Library are *Hurrah, We're Outward Bound!* (1968) and *And So My Garden Grows* (1969); all published by Doubleday.